EASY S

SPICY AND HEAL ___ ᴜᴋᴜᴍᴘ AND PRAWN RECIPES

JOSEPH VEEBE

Books in this Series:

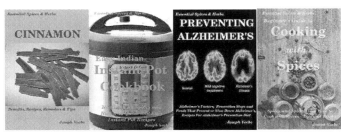

TABLE OF CONTENTS

CHAPTER 1. INTRODUCTION

INTRODUCTION

This is the 3rd book on the "Easy Spicy Recipes" series. As explained in the previous books, spices and herbs have a long and proven history of effective use as a flavoring ingredient in food preparations as well as medicinal use in potions, tinctures, and other alternative therapies.

Shrimp is one of the easiest and fastest protein to cook. It can be boiled, steamed, roasted, fried, saluted, baked, grilled, or barbequed in 5 minutes or less. You can use them in omelets, salsa, quiche, savory pastries, and many other dishes as well.

The recipes in the book combine the natural goodness of shrimp with healing properties of spices and herbs and create wholesome, healthy, anti-inflammatory, and disease-fighting recipe ideas.

The recipes in the book are put together so that they can be easily prepared using ingredients that are wholesome, natural, and commonly available. There are several optional ingredients that you can try out to make the dish according to your taste and creativity.

This book contains primarily shrimp and prawn preparations that are spicy and using common spices and herbs. Shrimp recipes that do not use spices are not part of this book.

While the author loves cooking for his family, he does not like to follow a strict prescription for cooking or recipes. He believes in spending as little time in the kitchen as possible while preparing natural, healthy, and tasty food. He likes to be creative and try out various ingredients to do not like to follow strict measurements.

HEALTH BENEFITS OF SPICES

Spices and herbs used in recipes described in this book have many health benefits. Some of them are listed below:

- Antioxidant properties
- Anti-inflammatory properties
- Anti-cancer properties
- Anti-fungal, anti-microbial, anti-viral
- Help the immune system and fight infections.
- Lower blood pressure
- Lower cholesterol
- Lower diabetes
- Improve circulation.
- And many others

Spices and herbs, if used correctly, could improve overall health and help fight many health conditions in a natural and supplemental fashion to modern treatments.

DIFFERENCE BETWEEN PRAWN AND SHRIMP

I have used prawn and shrimp interchangeably throughout this book. You can substitute shrimp with prawn in almost all of the recipes in the book. In terms of nutritional profile, both shrimp and prawn are almost identical too. So, you may ask, what is the difference between shrimp and prawn?

The answer to that question depends on a number of factors such as regions or countries where shrimp/prawn terms are being used, the habitat of these creatures, their anatomy, and their size among others.

Factors	Prawn vs Shrimp
UK, Australia, New Zealand, Ireland, India (most commonwealth countries	The general term used is prawn and it usually refers to both shrimp and true prawn
North America	The general term used is shrimp. Prawn is used occasionally to describe the larger variety of either, usually caught or farmed from fresh water.
Scientific names	Both prawn and shrimp come from different branches of the crustacean family and therefore they are considered scientifically distinct. Shrimp belongs to the *pleocyemata* suborder (which includes crayfish, lobster and crab) while prawns belong to the *dendrobranchiate* suborder.
Anatomy	Both Shrimp and Prawns are exoskeletons. The body is divided

	into three parts, head, thorax, and abdomen.
	Thorax in shrimp overlaps the head and abdomen and allows shrimp's body to be more flexible such as bending their body sharply compared to prawns.
	Prawns usually have 3 pairs of claw-like legs while shrimp has one pair of claw-like legs. Prawns legs are longer.
	Another anatomical difference is that while shrimp carry their fertilized eggs underside of their body, prawns release their eggs into the water to hatch and grow.
Habitat	Most Prawns are fresh-water species. Shrimp can be found in both fresh and salt-water.
	Prawns prefer warm waters while shrimp can be found in both cold and warm water.
Size	Prawns tend to be larger in size (such as tiger prawn) while shrimp are usually smaller.

NUTRITIONAL PROFILE OF SHRIMP AND PRAWN

Both shrimp and prawn have a similar nutritional profile. If you love shrimp, know that shrimp is one of the healthiest foods.

100 grams (3.5 oz) of shrimp / prawn provides the following:

- 20 grams of protein
- 100 calories
- 340 mg of omega-3 fatty acids
- 190 mg of cholesterol
- About 60% daily value of high-quality selenium (easily absorbed by body)
- Good source of B12, Iron and phosphorous

NOTES ON RECIPES IN THIS BOOK

Recipes in this book are not a collection of authentic dishes, but a spicy version of shrimp/prawn recipes that are easy to make and 100% healthy and flavorful. Ingredients used are mostly natural without any preserved or processed foods. Most of these recipes include tips and tricks to vary and adapt to your taste as well as your tolerance of spice levels. You can also substitute ingredients you like and skip the ones you don't like.

There are about 25 recipes in the book with ideas to make another 25 or even more with the suggestions and notes included with many of the recipes. Cooking does not have to be prescriptive but can be creative. If you are like me who does not want to spend a lot of time in the kitchen but love to cook healthy, natural, and wholesome food, this book is for you. I invite you to try your own variations and apply your creativity to cook dishes that are truly your own. Please see my book "Beginner's Guide to Cooking with Spices" to find out many health benefits of individual spices and also tips and tricks in using these.

CHAPTER 2. BAKED, GRILLED AND FRIED SHRIMP

TANDOORI PRAWN

Tandoori prawn is an easy and quick recipe where fresh prawn marinated in spices and grilled or baked in the oven. Can be served as an appetizer or finger food at parties.

Ingredients

- 1 lb. peeled, deveined, and washed prawns
- 2 tablespoon olive oil
- 1 teaspoon turmeric powder
- 1-2 teaspoon chili powder
- 1 teaspoon ginger-garlic paste
- ½ tsp salt or to taste
- 2 tablespoon lemon juice

Method

1. Mix all the ingredients in a bowl. Add prawn. Mix well and marinate for 1 hour or overnight.
2. Grill the prawn on a skewer for about 5 minutes each side or until cooked through.

Recipe Notes:

1. Depending on your spice tolerance level, you can adjust chili powder and garam masala to make it mild, medium, or hot.
2. If you like, you can skip most of the spice powders except turmeric and black pepper powder.

SPICY BAKED SHRIMP #1

Ingredients

- 2 tablespoon Worcestershire sauce
- 2 teaspoon fresh ground pepper
- ½ teaspoon turmeric powder
- 1-2 teaspoon chili powder
- 2 teaspoon ginger-garlic paste
- ½-1 tsp salt or to taste
- 2 tablespoon lemon juice
- 4 tablespoons of extra virgin olive oil
- ¼ cup fresh chopped cilantro
- 1 lbs. peeled, deveined, washed shrimp, tail on
- 1 lemon sliced thin

Method

1. Pre-heat oven to 400 degrees (about 200 degrees Celsius).
2. Mix the first 9 ingredients in a bowl.
3. Layer shrimp and lemon slices in a 9x9 baking dish.
4. Pour the sauce from the step 2 on top of the shrimp.
5. Bake for about 10-12 minutes or until shrimp turns pink. Gently stir with a spoon (or fork) at about 6 minutes.

Serve shrimp with French bread and the sauce from baking.

Recipe Notes:

1. Try with and without chili powder and see which one you like better.
2. Try different herbs instead of cilantro – basil, mint, parsley. Each one will offer a different flavor.

SPICY BAKED SHRIMP #2

This recipe mixes spices with Cajun spice and soy sauce instead of Worcester sauce.

Ingredients

- 1 lb. peeled, deveined, washed shrimp, tail on
- 2 tablespoon olive oil
- 1 teaspoon turmeric powder
- 1 teaspoon chili powder
- 1 teaspoon Cajun spice
- ½ tsp salt or to taste
- 2 tablespoon soy sauce
- 2 tablespoon lemon juice
- ¼ cup fresh chopped parsley

Method

1. Mix all the ingredients in a bowl. Add shrimp. Mix well and marinate for 1 hour or overnight.

2. Pre-heat oven to 400 degrees (about 200 degrees Celsius).
3. Arrange shrimp on baking pan. Discard any left-over marinade. Bake for about 10 minutes turning over prawns at 5 minutes.

Serve with French bread.

Recipe Notes:
As in the previous recipe -
1. Try with and without chili powder and see which one you like better.
2. Try different herbs instead of cilantro – basil, mint, parsley. Each one will offer a different flavor.

SPICY CRISPY PRAWN FRY

Ingredients

- 2 lbs. large prawn peeled and deveined
- ½ - 1 tsp cumin powder (optional)
- 2-3 tsp Kashmiri chili powder
- ½ tsp turmeric
- 2-3 tsp coriander powder
- 1-2 tsp garam masala
- 2 tsp ginger-garlic paste
- Salt to taste
- ½ cup oil to fry shrimp
- ½ cup corn flour
- 1 jalapeno – finely diced (optional)
- 1 tbsp minced curry leaves (optional)

- 1 tbsp minced coriander leaves (optional)

Method

1. In a large enough bowl, mix all the ingredients (except oil). Marinate for 5-6 hours or overnight.
2. Heat oil in frying pan and fry the marinated shrimp for about 6-8 minutes on both sides till the shrimp is brown and crispy.
3. Serve with your favorite chutney or tomato ketchup.

Recipe Notes:

1. You can adjust the amount of spice to control the spice/heat level.
2. You can try one or more of the optional ingredients.
3. You can add 1 tbsp lemon juice or vinegar while marinating.

SPICY ROASTED SHRIMP

Ingredients

- 1-1/2 lbs. large peeled, deveined shrimp
- 2 tablespoon olive oil
- 1 teaspoon turmeric powder
- 1 teaspoon chili powder
- 1 teaspoon Cajun spice

Method

1. Toss the shrimp with oil and spices.
2. Pre-heat oven to 400 degrees (about 200 degrees Celsius).
3. Arrange shrimp on a cooking sheet. Roast for about 10 minutes until cooked through.

Serve with any dipping sauce, tartar sauce, tomato ketchup or cocktail sauce.

Recipe Notes:
1. Try some herbs with this recipe- cilantro, basil, mint, parsley. Each one will offer a different flavor.

CHAPTER 3. SHRIMP MASALA, SHRIMP CURRY AND SHRIMP STIR-FRY

8-10 MINUTE SHRIMP MASALA

This is one of the quickest ways you can make spicy shrimp. There are not may ingredients (if you decide not to use optional ones) and can be made in about 10 minutes.

Basic Ingredients

- 1 lbs. large shrimp, peeled and deveined
- 2 cups of medium salsa
- 1 teaspoon chili powder
- ½ teaspoon turmeric powder
- 1 teaspoon coriander powder
- 1 teaspoon grated ginger (optional)
- 3-5 cloves of minced garlic (optional)
- 2 tablespoon olive or coconut oil
- ¼ cup chopped cilantro/parsley (optional)

Method

1. Heat oil, sauté spice powders for about 30 seconds. Add optional ginger and garlic. Make sure spices do not burn.
2. Add salsa. Mix well.
3. Add shrimp. Mix well so shrimp is coated with the spices. Cover and cook for 3-4 minutes on medium heat or shrimp is cooked.
4. Sprinkle optional cilantro before serving.

Serve with rice or bread.

Recipe Notes:
1. Instead of individual spices, you can try 1-2 tsp fish curry masala (available in South Asian stores), curry powder or garam masala. As you can expect, each one will give you slightly differently flavored/spiced 10-minute shrimp masala.
2. Try different herbs instead of cilantro – basil, mint, parsley. Each one will offer a different flavor.
3. Try adding one spring of curry leaves at the end of step one (careful not to splatter hot oil). This will give distinct curry leaf flavor and aroma.
4. You can also chop up 1 medium onion and sauté it in step 1 before adding ginger and garlic.

SHRIMP STIR FRY WITH GARLIC AND GINGER #1

Basic Ingredients

- 1 lb. large shrimp, peeled and deveined
- 1 teaspoon chili powder
- ½ teaspoon turmeric powder
- ½ teaspoon salt or to taste
- 2 teaspoon grated ginger
- 6 cloves of minced garlic
- 1 cup chopped up green onions
- 3 tablespoon olive or coconut oil
- ¼ cup chopped cilantro/parsley/basil

Method

1. First, remove any excess water from the shrimp by patting it with a paper towel. Now sprinkle chili powder, turmeric, and salt on top of shrimp and mix well. Let it marinate for 20 minutes.
2. Heat 2 tbsp oil and fry the shrimp for about 2-3 minutes on both sides. The spices will stick to the shrimp and it will be half cooked.
3. Remove shrimp and the add rest of the oil. Sauté onions, ginger, and garlic. Now add the shrimp and stir well and cook for another 1-2 minutes or until shrimp is cooked through.
4. Sprinkle optional the herbs of your choice, mix well, and your shrimp is ready.

Serve with rice or bread.

SHRIMP STIR FRY WITH GARLIC AND GINGER #2

This is a milder version of earlier shrimp stir fry. Jalapenos or green chilies may be added if you like to spice up a bit more.

Basic Ingredients

- 1 lb. large shrimp, peeled and deveined
- 1 teaspoon chili powder
- ½ teaspoon turmeric powder
- ½ teaspoon salt or to taste
- 2 teaspoon grated ginger
- 6 cloves of minced garlic
- 1 cup chopped up green onions
- 3 tablespoon olive or coconut oil

- ¼ cup chopped cilantro/parsley/basil

Method

1. First, remove any excess water from the shrimp by patting it with a paper towel. Now sprinkle chili powder, turmeric, and salt on top of shrimp and mix well. Let it marinate for 20 minutes.
2. Heat 2 tbsp oil and fry the shrimp for about 2-3 minutes on both sides. The spices will stick to the shrimp and it will be half cooked.
3. Remove shrimp and add the rest of the oil. Sauté onions, ginger, and garlic. Now add the shrimp and stir well and cook for another 1-2 minutes or until shrimp is cooked through.
4. Sprinkle optional the herbs of your choice, mix well, and your shrimp is ready.

Serve with rice or bread.

SHRIMP BUTTER ROAST

Basic Ingredients

- 2 lbs. large shrimp peeled and deveined
- 2 medium red onion sliced thin
- 1 tablespoon grated ginger
- 4-6 cloves of garlic chopped
- 3-4 tomatoes chopped
- 1-2 tsp chili powder
- 1-2 tsp coriander powder

- 1 tsp turmeric powder
- 1-2 tsp garam masala/curry powder
- ½ teaspoon black pepper powder
- ½ tsp salt or to taste
- 2 tablespoon lemon juice
- 2 tablespoon butter
- 1-2 tablespoon coconut/olive oil
- 2 spring curry leaves/ ½ cup cilantro
- 1 lemon cut into wedges
- 1-2 tablespoon vinegar (optional)

Method

1. Mix the shrimp with ½ tsp turmeric, salt, 2 tablespoon lemon juice and set aside to marinate for 10-15 minutes.
2. Add 2 tablespoon butter and fry the marinated prawns both sides for about 1-2 minutes. Remove the prawn and set aside.
3. In the same pan, add oil. Add garlic, ginger and onions. Add chili powder, coriander powder, turmeric, and garam masala. Sauté for about 30 seconds. Now add tomatoes and curry leaves/coriander leaves. Mix well and cook for 2-3 minutes or until the tomatoes are wilted.
4. Add fried shrimp. Mix well. Add 1/4 – ½ cup water if required. Cover and cook for another 2-3 minutes or until any residual water is evaporated and shrimp is cooked.
5. Add additional vinegar or lemon juice and salt to your liking and serve.

Recipe Notes:

1. Depending on your spice tolerance level, you can adjust chili powder and garam masala to make it mild, medium, or hot.
2. If you like, you can skip most of the spice powders except turmeric and black pepper powder.
3. Try making it without tomatoes and see if you like that better than one with tomatoes.
4. Instead of tomatoes, you could use tomato paste.
5. Instead of curry leaves/ cilantro, you could try other herbs such as parsley, basil, or thyme. Each one will give a different flavor/taste.

PRAWN ROAST WITH COCONUT CHIPS

This recipe is similar to the one above but a little more elaborate and also uses generous amount of coconut chips. This recipe also uses large prawns (such as tiger prawn). If you are a fan of coconut and shrimp, this is a must-try.

Basic Ingredients

- 2 lbs. large shrimp peeled and deveined
- 2 tsp ginger-garlic paste
- 1-2 tsp chili powder
- 1-2 tsp coriander powder
- 1 tsp turmeric powder
- 1-2 tsp garam masala/curry powder
- ½-1 teaspoon black pepper powder
- ½ tsp salt or to taste
- 3-4 tomatoes chopped
- 2 medium red onion sliced thin
- 2-3 tablespoon coconut/olive oil

- 2 spring curry leaves/ ½ cup cilantro
- 1 cup coconut chips

Method

1. Combine the prawn with ½ measures of chili powder, turmeric, black pepper powder, salt, and ginger-garlic paste and mix well and set aside for 15 min – 1 hr.
2. Add 2 tablespoon oil and fry the marinated prawns both sides for about 1-2 minutes. If you are using curry leaves, have them fry in oil along with prawns. Oil fried curry leaves give flavor and aroma to the prawns. Remove the prawn and set aside.
3. In the same pan, add the rest of the oil. Fry coconut chips until they are golden brown. Add onions, ginger-garlic paste, and sauté. Add the rest of the chili powder, coriander powder, turmeric, and garam masala. Sauté for about 30 seconds. Now add tomatoes. Mix well and cook for 2-3 minutes or until the tomatoes are wilted.
4. Add fried shrimp. Mix well. Cook for 2-3 minutes stirring occasionally until residual water is evaporated.
5. Add additional salt, if needed. Mix well and serve.

Recipe Notes:

1. Depending on your spice tolerance level, you can adjust chili powder and garam masala to make it mild, medium, or hot.
2. If you like, you can add whole red chilies, split green chilies/jalapenos and additional curry leaves while frying coconut chips in step 2. This will make it a bit more spicy but flavorful.

3. Instead of tomatoes, you could use tomato paste.
4. You can add chopped up cilantro/parsley in step 5.
5. Coconut chips may be made from cracking open a fresh coconut and using a knife to carve out chips or buy dried or frozen coconut chips from grocery stores.
6. This recipe is similar to a recipe given later in this book.

Mango Shrimp

Ingredients

- 1 lb. shrimp peeled
- Chili powder 1-2 tsp (depending on your tolerance level)
- turmeric ½ tsp
- Coriander powder- ½ tbsp
- Fenugreek powder-1/4 tsp or fenugreek seeds ½ tsp (optional)
- Black pepper powder- ¼ tsp
- Mustard seeds-1/2 tsp
- 1 medium onion
- Grated ginger 2 tsp
- Crushed garlic 4-5 cloves
- Curry leaves-2 sprigs (optional)
- Washed and cut green mango (with skin or skin removed depending on your preference) – 1 cup
- Water-1 to 1.5 cups(or as required)
- Salt to taste
- 2-4 sliced green chilies or jalapeños, seeds removed (optional)

Method

1. Combine all the spices powders – chili, turmeric, coriander, fenugreek, and pepper powder together in a bowl. Add 2 tsp or just enough water to make a thick paste and set aside.
2. Heat oil in a pan and splutter mustard seeds and fenugreek (if seeds used instead of powder).
3. Add ginger, garlic, onions, optional green chilies, and curry leaves. Sauté until onion becomes translucent.
4. Add the masala paste and mix well on low flame (Wet the masala to make sure it gets fried but not burnt).
5. After about 30 seconds (once masala gets fried), add about 1 cup of water mix and then add the cut mango pieces.
6. Cover it and bring it a boil on medium heat (about 3-4 minutes). By now mango pieces should become tender. Add shrimp. Mix gently.
7. Cover the pan and cook it for about 8-12 minutes or until shrimp is cooked and the gravy is thick. Switch off the flame and keep it covered for 30 minutes for the shrimp to soak in the spices and mango flavor.

Serve with rice or bread.

Notes:

1. Paprika may be used instead of chili powder if you desire to make it less spicy.

2. Prawns may be used instead of shrimp.
3. ½-1 cup coconut milk may be added in step 7. In this case, reduce the amount of water added in step 5.
4. Cut tomatoes may be added along with mango in step 5 for a variation of this recipe.
5. You can try making the same recipe with ripe mangos. This will be savory, sweet, and sour dish due to the spices and ripe mango.

EASY THAI RED CURRY SHRIMP

Ingredients

- 1-1/2 lbs. peeled, deveined and washed shrimp
- 1-2 tbsp coconut oil
- 1 tbsp ginger-garlic paste
- ¼ cup or 4 tbsp red curry paste
- 1 can of coconut milk
- ¼ cup Thai basil chopped
- 2 Lime leaves

Method

1. Heat oil in a large pan over medium heat, sauté ginger-garlic paste for about a minute. Add Thai red curry paste and mix for another minute.
2. Add coconut milk and bring it a boil.

3. Add shrimp and lime leaves. Bring to a boil and simmer covered for 8-10 minutes or until shrimp is cooked.
4. Add Thai basil. Mix. Switch off the heat. Keep it covered for a couple of minutes before serving.

Recipes Notes:

Below are some of the ideas to make three or four different versions of the Thai shrimp curry.

1. You can try adding 1 tsp soy sauce and/or 1 tsp vinegar. Should you like the taste you can make it as part of the recipe.
2. Try adding ½ teaspoon fish sauce.
3. Try adding 1 tsp brown sugar and see if you like it. If you do, you can add it as part of the recipe.
4. You can add vegetables such as bell pepper or green beans. If you plan to add vegetables make sure to cook them to your liking prior to adding shrimp in step 3. Some of the vegetables may take more time to cook than shrimp.
5. You can make your own Thai red curry paste by following the recipe in my book "Introduction to Curry" or buy off the shelf from Asian or online stores.

THAI GREEN CURRY SHRIMP

Basic Ingredients

- 1.5 lbs. peeled, deveined and washed shrimp
- 1/2 cup Thai green curry paste
- 1 cup green beans (whole or cut into half)
- 1 cup broccoli
- 1 cup coconut milk
- ½ inch ginger, sliced into long pieces
- ½ cup cilantro
- 2 tsp coconut (or vegetable) oil
- 1 sliced green chili (optional)
- Salt to taste
- 1 tsp lime juice

Method

1. Heat oil in a non-stick pan, add the green curry paste, green chilies, and ginger, and fry it for 1-2 minutes stirring well.
2. Add beans and broccoli. Mix well. Cook for 5 minutes until beans and broccoli are tender. Now add shrimp and mix well.
3. Add coconut milk; cover and cook for 5-8 minutes or until the vegetables and shrimp are cooked. Add ½-1 cup chicken broth if required.
4. Garnish with cilantro and serve with Jasmine rice.

Notes:

1. You can use the green curry paste made using the recipes given in my book "Introduction to Curry" or buy off the shelf from Asian or online stores.

2. You can also add some lemongrass to enhance the flavor.

SPICY PICKLED SHRIMP/PRAWN

Indian and South Asian pickles are very spicy unlike the pickles in North America and Europe. The Asian pickle spice mix generally includes a generous amount of chili powder, turmeric, mustard seeds, fenugreek seeds, and asafetida. While spicy vegetable pickles are very popular, meat, fish, and shrimp can also be pickled. There are many ways to pickle shrimp. The idea is to soak marinated and fried shrimp in a sauce containing a lot of chili and other ingredients and vinegar. Pickle can last several weeks in the fridge and is consumed in moderation as they are really spicy.

Ingredients

- 1-1/2 lbs. small shrimp
- 4 tablespoon vegetable oil
- 1 cup finely chopped onions
- 2-4 tablespoon red chili powder
- 1 teaspoon turmeric powder
- 2-inch ginger piece finely chopped (or paste)
- 10-12 cloves of garlic chopped (or paste)
- 10 green chilies or jalapeno peppers chopped (optional)
- 2 spring curry leaves
- 1 teaspoon mustard seeds
- 1 teaspoon fenugreek seeds

- ½-1 cup vinegar (white/ red wine / rice wine/apple cider)
- ½ teaspoon salt or to taste
- 4-6 tablespoon oil

Method

1. Use 1 tablespoon chili powder, ½ teaspoon turmeric, 1 tablespoon vinegar, and salt to mix with the shrimp. Marinate for 30 minutes – 1 hr.
2. Heat 2-3 tablespoon oil and fry the marinated shrimp both sides for about 3-4 minutes or until shrimp is cooked. Remove the shrimp and set aside.
3. Add rest of the oil in the same pan, crackle mustard seeds, and fenugreek seeds. sauté onions, garlic, ginger, green chilies, and curry leaves for 1-2minutes. Add rest of the spices and mix for another 1-2 minutes or the spices are cooked.
4. Now add the fried shrimp. Mix well.
5. Add vinegar, cover and simmer for 1-2 minutes.
6. Add additional salt if required and mix. Let it cool down.
7. Transfer it into a glass jar and use it as a condiment to add flavor to your dishes or a side dish. It should last in the fridge for at least a month.

Recipe notes:
1. Though vegetable oil is used in the recipe as it is easier to buy, mustard oil is the best oil to make spicy pickles.
2. There are several alternative ways to make this pickle and each may come out a bit different than the recipe given above.
3. Instead of frying the shrimp in oil, you could bake it or air fry it, before mixing with the pickle masala

4. The same recipe may be tried without marinating in the interest of time and you can get similar results.
5. You could substitute 2-3 tablespoons of lemon juice instead of vinegar.
6. Try the same recipe with different vinegar and see how you like it.
7. Since this dish can be kept for a long time in the fridge and is only used as a side in moderation, care must be taken every time you use a spoon to take pickle, the spoon needs to be dry and clean or the pickle could go bad.

SHRIMP/PRAWN 65

Shrimp/Prawn 65 is a deep-fried shrimp dish that can be eaten as an appetizer or as part of a meal.

Ingredients

- 2 lbs. large shrimp peeled and deveined
- ½ - 1 tsp cumin powder
- 2-3 tsp Kashmiri chili powder
- ½ tsp turmeric
- 2-3 tsp coriander powder
- ½ tsp black pepper powder
- 2 tsp ginger-garlic paste
- Salt to taste
- ½ cup oil to fry shrimp
- ½ cup corn flour
- 2 egg whites

- ½ cup tomato sauce
- 5-6 garlic cloves chopped
- 1 tsp grated ginger
- 3-4 jalapenos chopped (optional)
- 2 tbsp coconut or olive oil
- 2-3 whole red chilies (optional)
- 1 spring curry leaves (optional)

Method

1. In a large enough bowl, mix Kashmiri chili powder, coriander powder, turmeric powder, pepper powder, salt, ginger-garlic paste, egg white and corn flour. Add shrimp and mix it well so the shrimp is coated with the marinade. Marinate for 5-6 hours or overnight.
2. Heat oil in frying pan and shallow fry the marinated shrimp on both sides till the shrimp is brown and crispy. Set these fried shrimps aside.
3. Heat 2 tbsp oil in a large enough pan (the same pan used for frying shrimp may be used), sauté garlic, ginger, jalapenos, whole red chilies and curry leaves. Add fried shrimp and tomato sauce. Toss well for a minute.
4. Switch off the heat. Garnish with chopped green onions or cilantro and/or lemon wedges and serve.

Recipe Notes:

1. You can adjust the amount of spices to control the spice/heat level

2. Instead of curry leaves, you may use cilantro.
3. You can try making this without using corn flour.
4. Try making it without tomato sauce and add 1 tablespoon of lemon juice instead and see if you like it better.
5. You can add lemon juice or vinegar while marinating.
6. For those who want this even more spicy, try adding 1-2 chili powder and/or 1-2 chili sauce in step 3.
7. Instead of shrimp, large prawns may be used.
8. If you are like me and don't want to spend too much time in the kitchen, you can just ignore steps 3 & 4 and enjoy the fried shrimp from step 2. This should be still pretty good.

GINGER PRAWNS

Ingredients

- 2 lbs. large shrimp peeled and deveined
- ½ - 1 curry powder/garam masala powder
- 1 tsp ginger-garlic paste
- ½ tsp turmeric
- ½ tsp black pepper powder
- ½ tsp salt
- ½ cup oil to fry shrimp

- 2-inch ginger piece grated (2-3 tsp)
- 5-6 garlic cloves diced

- 1 medium red onion finely chopped
- 1-2 tsp red chili paste
- 1-2 tablespoon soy sauce
- 2 tbsp coconut or olive oil
- 2-3 whole red chilies (optional)
- ½ cup cilantro minced (optional)
- 2 tablespoon vinegar
- 2 tablespoon corn flour (optional)

Method

1. In a large enough bowl, mix garam masala powder, turmeric powder, pepper powder, and salt. Add shrimp and mix it well so the shrimp is coated with the marinade. Set aside for 1 hr.
2. Heat oil in frying pan and shallow fry the marinated shrimp on both sides till the shrimp is brown and crispy. Set these fried shrimps aside.
3. Heat 2 tbsp oil in a large enough pan (the same pan used for frying shrimp may be used), sauté garlic, ginger, onion, whole red chilies and cilantro. Add fried shrimp. Toss well for a minute. Now add vinegar and optional corn flour mixed in ½ cup hot water.
4. Stir well, cover and cook for 1-2 minutes stirring in between, Switch off the heat.

Recipe Notes:

1. You can adjust the amount of spices to control the spice/heat level

2. Instead of curry leaves, you may use cilantro.
3. You can try making this without using corn flour.
4. Instead of using chopped up onion, ginger and garlic in step 3, optionally you may puree then and add. This will be almost like a different dish.
5. You can add lemon juice or vinegar while marinating.
6. For those who want this even more spicy, try adding 1-2 tsp chili powder and in step 3.
7. Instead of shrimp, large prawns may be used.
8. **You** can vary the proportion of ginger and garlic to get either more **ginger-flavored prawn (ginger prawn)** or more **garlic-flavored prawn (garlic prawn).** Just use your imagination and you can make several variations of this recipe. This is true for most recipes in this book.

SPICY PRAWNS MASALA/ROAST

Basic Ingredients

- 2 lbs. large shrimp, peeled and deveined
- 3-5 teaspoon chili powder
- 2 tsp Kashmiri chili powder
- 2-3 tsp coriander powder
- 1-2 teaspoon turmeric powder
- ½ teaspoon salt or to taste
- 1-2 tsp grated ginger or ginger paste
- 1-2 tsp minced garlic or garlic paste
- 2-3 tomatoes chopped

- 2 medium onions chopped
- 1-2 jalapenos or green chilies sliced (optional)
- 2 tablespoon olive or coconut oil
- 2 spring curry leaves

Method

1. Sprinkle 1-2 tsp chili powder, ½ tsp turmeric, and salt on top of shrimp and mix well. Let it marinate for 20 minutes.
2. Heat 3 tbsp oil and sauté onions, garlic, ginger, jalapenos, and curry leaves. Add all the rest of the spices (go easy on spices if your tolerance level is low). Mix well for about 30 seconds so spices get cooked. Now add tomatoes and mix. Cover and cook for about 2 minutes mixing well.
3. Add marinated shrimp. Stir well so the shrimp is well coated with spices. Add ½ cup water or just enough for the shrimp to cook. Cover and cook for 5-8 minutes or until the shrimp are cooked through.
4. Sprinkle optional the herbs of your choice, mix well, adjust/add salt, and your shrimp is ready.

Serve with rice or bread.

Recipe Notes:
1. This recipe is very spicy. You can adjust the amount of spices to control the spice/heat level
2. Instead of curry leaves, you may use cilantro.
3. Instead of using chopped up onion, ginger, and garlic in step 3, optionally you may puree then and add. This will be almost like a different dish.
4. You can add lemon juice or vinegar while marinating.

5. You could fry the marinated shrimp in 2-3 tbsp oil before step 2 and use the fried shrimp in step 3. In this case, you do not need 5-8 minutes to cook the shrimp. 2-3 minutes to mix well with the spices will be enough. This will also taste differently from the recipe without frying.
6. Instead of shrimp, large prawns may be used.

SPICY PRAWNS MASALA/ROAST WITH COCONUT

You may have tried coconut-crusted shrimp where most recipes follow the four step process of 1) shrimp is coated with flour, 2) beaten egg and then 3) coconut flakes+ panko bread crumb mix and then 4) fried in oil. You can convert this into somewhat a spicy dish by marinating shrimp in some spice combination as in one of the dishes in the book before coating with flour and following rest of the steps.

The recipe below is entirely different from the many different recipes available for coconut-crusted shrimp. Here coconut chips (thinly sliced and about ½ inch long) are toasted in oil and used in making the spicy prawn roast. Most of the ingredients for this recipe is the same as the previous recipe. Toasted coconut gives a unique flavor and good crunch.

Basic Ingredients

- All the same ingredients as in the previous recipe.
- 1-2 cup toasted coconut chips.

Method

1. Heat 1 tbsp oil in a pan and add coconut chips. Toast them for a few minutes until they become golden in color. Remove the toasted coconut chips and set aside. The same pan may be used for the next step.
2. Follow steps 1 and 2 as in the previous recipe. Add toasted coconut chips along with shrimp in step 3 and follow the rest of the steps as above.

Serve with rice or bread.

Recipe Notes:

1. Coconut chips may be bought as frozen or dried form. If you are using frozen coconut chips, thaw it before frying. Of course, you can buy fresh coconut and make chips as well.
2. All other recipe notes for the previous recipe apply to this one as well.
3. If you are fan of coconut, roasted coconut chips may be added some of the other recipes as well, especially those ones which are dry dishes without much sauce.

PRAWN CURRY WITH COCONUT MILK

Basic Ingredients

- 2 lbs. large shrimp, peeled and deveined
- 2-4 teaspoon chili powder

- 1-2 tsp curry powder / garam masala powder
- 1easpoon turmeric powder
- ½ teaspoon salt or to taste
- 1-2 tsp grated ginger or ginger paste
- 1-2 tsp minced garlic or garlic paste
- 2-3 tomatoes chopped
- 2 medium onions chopped
- 1-2 jalapenos or green chilies sliced (optional)
- 2 tablespoon olive or coconut oil
- 2 spring curry leaves
- 1 can coconut milk

Method

1. Heat 3 tbsp oil and sauté onions, garlic, ginger, jalapenos, and curry leaves. Once the onions become translucent, add all of the spices (go easy on spices if your tolerance level is low). Mix well for about 30 seconds so spices get cooked. Now add tomatoes and mix. Cover and cook for about 2-3 minutes mixing well.
2. Add shrimp. Stir well so the shrimp is well coated with spices. Keep stirring for about 2-3 minutes so shrimp gets partially cooked. Now add the coconut milk, mix well and cover and cook for 5-8 minutes on low heat or until the shrimp are cooked through.
3. Sprinkle optional the herbs of your choice, mix well, adjust/add salt, and your shrimp is ready.

Serve with rice or bread.

Recipe Notes:
1. This recipe is very spicy. You can adjust the amount of spices to control the spice/heat level

Easy Spicy Shrimp   41

2. Instead of curry leaves, you may use cilantro.
3. Instead of using chopped up onion, ginger, and garlic in step 3, optionally you may puree then and add. This will be almost like a different dish.
4. You can add lemon juice or vinegar while marinating.
5. You could fry the marinated shrimp in 2-3 tbsp oil before step 2 and use the fried shrimp in step 3. In this case, you do not need 5-8 minutes to cook the shrimp. 2-3 minutes to mix well with the spices will be enough. This will also taste differently than the recipe without frying.
6. Instead of shrimp, large prawns may be used.

SHRIMP AND GREEN BEANS

This is a very simple recipe and quick to make. Shrimp and beans are an excellent combination and my mother used to make this recipe with fresh-caught shrimp/prawns and freshly harvested string beans from our vegetable patch.

Basic Ingredients

- 1 lb. shrimp or prawn
- 1 lb. beans cut into ½ inch-1 inch pieces
- 1 medium red onion chopped
- 4-5 garlic cloves chopped
- ½ teaspoon salt or to taste

- ½ tsp paprika
- 1-2 tsp chili powder
- ½ inch ginger grated (optional)
- ½ turmeric
- 1-2 jalapenos or green chilies sliced (optional)
- 2 tablespoon olive or coconut oil
- 1 tbsp lemon juice (optional)
- ½ cup water

Method

1. Heat oil in a pan, sauté onions, garlic, ginger, and jalapenos. Add spices and mix well for 30seconds – 1 minute until spices are cooked. Add a tablespoon water if needed so the spices do not get burned.
2. Add green beans. Mix well. Cover and cook for about 5 minutes or until the beans become tender.
3. Now add shrimp. Mix well. Cook covered on medium heat for another3-5 minutes or until shrimp is cooked and beans cooked to your desired level of tenderness. Add optional lemon juice, mix well and serve.

Recipe Notes:
1. Adjust the amount of chili powder to your spice/heat level
2. Try adding some herbs – curry leaves when you sauté onions or cilantro/parsley/basil towards the end of cooking.
3. Add tomatoes after sautéing onion along with beans.

4. If you are using large prawns, you can cut beans into an inch or inch and half sizes. If you are using small prawns, reduce the size of cut beans.
5. Frozen cut beans (regular cut or French cut) may be used instead of fresh beans.

PEPPER PRAWNS

Prawns and black peppers are a great combination and an easy dish to make. Here is the main spice is black pepper which slowly builds the spice and heat and the taste lingers on your lounge even after the dish is long gone.

Ingredients

- 1 lb. large shrimp deveined, shell on, head removed, washed
- 1 tablespoon ginger-garlic paste
- ½ tsp turmeric
- 1-2 tsp chili powder (optional)
- 2-3 tablespoon fresh black peppercorns coarsely ground
- ½ tsp salt
- 1 medium red onion finely chopped
- 1-2 tablespoon soy sauce
- 1-2 tablespoon oyster sauce
- 2 tbsp coconut or olive oil
- 2-3 whole red chilies (optional)
- 10 curry leaves (optional)

Method

1. Heat oil in a pan, sauté onions, ginger-garlic paste, red chilies, and curry leaves. Add turmeric and chili powder mix for 10-15 seconds. Now add ground pepper, oyster sauce, and soy sauce. Mix well.
2. Add prawn mix well so the prawns are coated well with the spices and gravy. Add a couple of tablespoon water, IF needed.
3. Cover and cook for 2-3 minutes or until prawns are cooked and water evaporates. Serve with rice.

Recipe Notes:

1. If you like to cut down the spice level, you can make this dish without any chili powder.
2. Instead of curry leaves, you may use cilantro.
3. Instead of using chopped up onion, ginger, and garlic in step 1, optionally you may puree then and add.
4. You can add lemon juice or vinegar in step 3.
5. You can make this dish with peeled prawns if you prefer.
6. You can garnish with cilantro or green onions in step 3.

CHAPTER 4. OTHER SHRIMP RECIPES

SHRIMP PASTA #1

Basic Ingredients

- 2 cup penne pasta
- ½ lb. shrimp
- ½ cup grated mozzarella cheese
- 1 tsp chili flakes
- 4-5 garlic cloves chopped
- ½ teaspoon salt or to taste
- ½ tsp paprika
- ¼ turmeric
- 1 cup sun-dried tomatoes
- 1-2 jalapenos or green chilies sliced (optional)
- 2 tablespoon olive or coconut oil
- ¼ cup basil
- ¼ cup milk
- ¼ cup fresh cream

Method

1. Heat water in a deep pan and boil pasta with salt and 1 tablespoon olive oil. Once cooked drain and keep aside.
2. Mix shrimp with salt, paprika, and turmeric and set aside for 10 minutes.

3. Heat oil in a pan, sauté garlic and jalapenos. Add shrimp and cook for 2-3 minutes. Remove shrimp and set aside.
4. Add sun-dried tomatoes in the same pan, add milk and cream and mix well. Boil on low-medium until the mixture is thick. Now add cheese, basil and chili flakes and mix well until it is creamy.
5. Add pasta and shrimp. Toss well and serve.

QUICK SPICY GARLIC SHRIMP PASTA/NOODLES #2

Basic Ingredients

- 1 lb./16 oz dried spaghetti pasta of your choice
- 1 lb. shrimp peeled and deveined
- 1 tsp red chili flakes
- 1-2 tsp chili powder
- 4-5 garlic cloves minced
- 1 medium red onion chopped
- 1-2 jalapenos or green chilies sliced (optional)
- 3 tablespoon olive oil
- 1 tablespoon butter
- 2 tablespoon chopped parsley or basil
- Salt and black pepper to taste

Method

1. Heat water in a deep pan and boil pasta with salt and 1 tablespoon olive oil. Once cooked drain and keep aside.
2. While pasta is cooking, heat oil in a pan, add butter, sauté onions, garlic, and jalapenos. Add chili powder and chili flakes and mix well. Add shrimp. Cook for 2-3 minutes.
3. Add pasta and parsley/basil and mix well and serve.

Recipe Notes:
1. If you like to vary the taste, you could use one or more of the following in step 2.
    a. 1-2 tbsp soy sauce
    b. ½ - 1 tbsp fish sauce
    c. 1-2 tsp chili sauce/paste
    d. ¼ - ½ tsp turmeric
2. Try adding the following vegetables in step 2.
    a. 3-5 green onions chopped
    b. ½ bell pepper thinly sliced – any color
3. You can skip the jalapenos in step 2 if you like.

SHRIMP SCAMPI

Shrimp scampi is a classic Italian dish of shrimp cooked with garlic, butter, white wine, and lemon. The dish is often served with spaghetti pasta.

Ingredients

- 1 lb. jumbo shrimp peeled and deveined
- 10 fresh garlic cloves chopped

- 1 tsp chili flakes
- ½ - 1 tsp freshly ground pepper
- ½ teaspoon salt or to taste
- 2 tbsp unsalted butter
- 2 tablespoon olive oil
- ½ cup white wine
- 1 lemon juiced
- ½ tsp lemon zest
- ½ lb. cooked spaghetti noodles

Method

1. Heat butter and olive oil in a large skillet. Sauté garlic for about 30 seconds to one minute
2. Add lemon zest, chili flakes, pepper, wine, and salt. Mix well. Simmer on low heat until the sauce is thickened and reduced to half.
3. Add shrimp and cook until pink. Stir well so both sides are cooked. About 2-4 minutes.
4. Add lemon juice and parsley. Mix well.
5. Serve over cooked spaghetti

Recipe Notes:
1. If you like this to be spicier, you can add one or two chopped up jalapenos in step 2.
2. Instead of serving over the cooked spaghetti, you could add the cooked spaghetti into the same skillet at the end of step 4 and mix well so spaghetti absorbs some of the flavor before serving.

LEMON-GARLIC SHRIMP

This is a lemon-flavored garlicky shrimp recipe. The lemon zest and lemon juice along with garlic and pepper should give this a nice taste. Jalapenos are optional if you like this to be more spicy. See the notes below for other creative ideas to tweak this recipe.

Basic Ingredients

- 1-1/2 lb. shrimp or prawn peeled and deveined
- 4-5 garlic cloves minced
- ½ teaspoon salt or to taste
- ½ inch ginger grated (optional)
- 1-2 jalapenos or green chilies sliced (optional)
- 2 tablespoon olive or coconut oil
- 1 stick or 4 tbsp butter
- Juice and zest from 1 lemon
- 1 tsp freshly ground pepper
- 2 tbsp basil or parsley
- ¼ cup water

Method

1. Heat oil in a pan. Add shrimp. Sprinkle salt and cook both sides until pink for about 2-3 minutes. Remove shrimp and set aside.
2. Add butter. Once melted add minced garlic, ginger, optional green chilies. Sauté until aromatic. Add lemon juice, lemon zest, and ¼ cup water. Stir well.
3. Add shrimp, toss well. Garnish with parsley and serve hot.

Recipe Notes:
1. Add ½ -1 tsp of chili flakes in step 3 for more kick.
2. Instead of jalapenos, you can add chili powder, chili sauce, or garam masala – this will give a different taste.
3. Try different herbs, basil, thyme, mint, or cilantro. Each will give a different flavor/taste.

SHRIMP FRIED RICE

Ingredients

- 1 lb. medium shrimp peeled and deveined
- 3-4 cups of cooked rice
- ½ tsp turmeric
- ½ black pepper powder
- ½ tsp salt or to taste
- 1 medium red onion finely chopped
- 2 tsp garlic paste
- ½ cup chicken/vegetable broth/ bone broth
- 1-2 tablespoon dark soy sauce
- 3 tbsp oil (sesame/olive/vegetable)
- 2-3 whole red chilies (optional)
- 1 cup bean sprouts (optional)
- ½ cup chopped scallions / green onions
- ½ tsp brown sugar (optional)
- 1 egg

Method

1. Add turmeric, pepper, and ¼ tsp salt to the shrimp. Mix well and set aside.
2. Heat 2 tbsp oil in a pan, fry shrimp on both sides for 2-3 minutes or until it becomes pink. Remove and set aside.
3. Add remaining oil into the same pan, sauté onions and garlic paste. Add optional bean sprouts and mix well. Add green onions.
4. Now move the ingredients in the pan to the sides to create some room to fry the egg. Add a bit of oil in the middle and crack the egg. Scramble it for 30 seconds and then mix everything together.
5. Now add the cooked rice. Mix well.
6. Mix chicken broth, soy sauce, and optional sugar all together in bowl and pour it over the rice.
7. Add fried shrimp. Mix well and your shrimp fried rice is ready.

Recipe Notes:

1. For most fried rice recipes, previously cooked rice (from the fridge or cooled down for many hours) is used as this will make the rice less soggy than using fresh rice.
2. You can add some peas and carrots in step 3, if you like.
3. You can skip sprouted beans if you choose.
4. You could also add 1 tsp fish sauce at the end of step 4.

5. Instead of frying/scrambling egg in step 4, egg may be fried/scrambled separately and added along with shrimp.
6. Instead of adding black pepper powder, you may add white pepper powder, onion powder, and or garlic powder in step 1 to marinate the shrimp.
7. You can garnish with cilantro or mint in step.

SPICY SHRIMP TACOS

Ingredients

- 1 lb. small shrimp cleaned and washed
- 1 tsp chili powder – divided
- ½ turmeric powder
- ½ tsp meat/garam masala (optional)
- ¼ cup red onions finely chopped
- ¼ cup cilantro chopped (optional)
- 1 cup Pico de gallo or salsa
- 1 avocado, peeled, seeded and diced
- 1 tbsp olive oil
- 12 flour tortillas
- Salt to taste
- Lime wedges

Method

1. Sprinkle ½ tsp chili powder and turmeric. Mix well and set aside.
2. Heat oil in a pan over medium heat, sauté onions, and spices.

3. Add shrimp and mix well so the spices with hot oil sticks to shrimp along with sautéed onions. Stir well and cook for 2-3 minutes. The small shrimps should get cooked pretty fast.
4. Warm tortillas, fill it with shrimp from step 3, top with avocado, Pico de gallo or salsa and cilantro and serve.

Recipe Notes:

1. You could also use medium or large shrimp to make tacos.
2. Shrimp may be fried in oil first and then added to sautéed onions in step 3.
3. You could spice this up even further by adding chopped up jalapenos in step 2.
4. You can add garlic and ginger as well as turmeric powder in step 2.
5. You can skip avocado entirely if you like.

KOREAN INSPIRED SPICY GARLIC SHRIMP

This is a sweet and spicy dish. If you like shrimp and like Korean, this is must try.

Ingredients

- 2 lbs. large shrimp/prawn cleaned, peeled, deveined
- ½ tsp turmeric

- ½ tsp chili powder
- ¼ cup red onions finely chopped
- 10-15 garlic cloves, chopped
- ¼ cup cilantro chopped (optional)
- 2-3 tbsp chili oil
- 2 tbsp oyster sauce
- 1-3 green chilies/jalapenos sliced (optional)
- 2-4 green onions chopped
- 1-2 tbsp chili flakes
- ½ -1 tsp black pepper powder
- 1-2 tbsp olive oil
- 2 tsp honey
- Salt to taste
- Lime wedges

Method

1. Sprinkle chili powder and turmeric on the shrimp. Mix well and set aside. In another bowl, mix oyster sauce, chili oil, chili flakes, and pepper powder and honey and set aside.
2. Heat oil in a pan over medium heat, sauté onions, and garlic. Add optional green chilies.
3. Add shrimp and mix well so the spices shrimp is coated with spice. Pour the oyster sauce, chili oil mixture. Mix well and cook for about 2-3 minutes.
4. Garnish with cilantro, green onions, and lemon wedges.

Recipe Notes:

1. You can add red or white wine in step 3 to deglaze the pan before adding the sauces.

2. You can add soy sauce and/or fish sauce and see how you like it.
3. You can skip honey if do not like the sweetness. You can also use one tablespoon brown sugar instead of honey.

GENERAL TIPS FOR COOKING SHRIMP

1. Shrimp and prawns cook pretty fast; about 3-4 minutes or less. If you cook more, the prawn could become chewy.
2. The spices you can use with shrimp or prawn limited by your creativity and imagination. Mix and match the spices as you like. Chili powder, turmeric, and black pepper powder goes really well with prawns. Other spices or spice mixes can be used according to your taste.
3. I have used turmeric, ginger and garlic in most of the recipes. In my opinion, these three spices are fundamental spices and offer a lot of healing power and make the dish very healthy. I have written separate books on these spices as they are so important in healthy food preparations.
4. Shrimp generates water while cooking. So, if you like your dish to be dry and not saucy, you may want to pat down the shrimp prior to cooking.
5. If you are adding vegetables to shrimp, cook them first so that it becomes tender before adding shrimp. This is true when using shrimp with other

ingredients as well. Add shrimp mostly towards the end of cooking.

6. While I have described most recipes as using peeled, deveined shrimp, if you prefer, you can use shrimp with shells in these recipes.

7. If you are frying shrimp first as given in some of the recipes, turn them over after 1-2 minutes on each side.

8. If you are buying packaged shrimp instead of fresh shrimp from the market, make sure to wash them in running water. Some of the packaged/frozen shrimp are chemically treated for shelf life.

DISCLAIMER

This book details the author's personal experiences in using Indian spices, the information contained in public domain as well as the author's opinion. The author is not licensed as a doctor, nutritionist, or chef. The author is providing this book and its contents on an "as is" basis and makes no representations or warranties of any kind with respect to this book or its contents. The author disclaims all such representations and warranties, including for example warranties of merchantability and educational or medical advice for a particular purpose. In addition, the author does not represent or warrant that the information accessible via this book is accurate, complete, or current. The statements made about products and services have not been evaluated by the US FDA or any equivalent organization in other countries.

The author will not be liable for damages arising out of or in connection with the use of this book or the information contained within. This is a comprehensive limitation of liability that applies to all damages of any kind, including (without limitation) compensatory; direct, indirect or consequential damages; loss of data, income or profit; loss of or damage to property and claims of third parties. It is understood that this book is not intended as a substitute for consultation with a licensed medical or a culinary professional. Before starting any lifestyle changes, it is recommended that you consult a licensed professional to ensure that you are doing what's best for your situation. The use of this book implies your acceptance of this disclaimer.

Thank You

If you enjoyed this book or found it useful, I would greatly appreciate if you could post a short review on Amazon. I read all the reviews and your feedback will help me to make this book even better.

COOKING MEASUREMENTS AND CONVERSION CHARTS

Some of you may be using a different kitchen measurement system than described in the book. I believe most people can navigate these different systems. The following conversion tables included as a ready reference; in case you need it.

US Dry Volume Measurements	
Measurement	**Equivalent**
3 teaspoons	1 Tablespoon
¼ cup	4 Tablespoons
1/3 cup	5 1/3 Tablespoons
½ cup	8 Tablespoons
¾ cup	12 Tablespoons
1 cup	16 Tablespoons
1 Pound	16 ounces

US Liquid Volume Measurements and Conversion	
8 Fluid ounces	1 Cup
1 Pint	2 Cups (or 16 fluid ounces)
1 Quart	2 Pints (or 4 cups)
1 Gallon	4 Quarts (or 16 cups)

US to Metric Conversions	
1 teaspoon	5 ml
1 tablespoon	15 ml

1 fluid oz.	30 ml
1 cup	240 ml
2 cups (1 pint)	470 ml
4 cups (1 quart)	940 ml or approx. 1 litre
4 quarts (1 gal.)	3.8 liters or 16 cups
1 oz.	28 grams
1 pound (16 Oz.)	454 grams or approx. ½ kilo gram

Metric to US Conversions	
100 ml	3.4 fluid oz.
240 ml	1 cup
1 liter	34 fluid oz./ 4.2 cups/2.1 Pints/1.06 quarts/0.26 gallon
100 grams	3.5 ounces
500 grams	1.10 pounds
1 kilogram	2.205 pounds or 35 oz.

Oven Temperature Conversions	
Fahrenheit	Celsius
275° F	140° C
300° F	150° C
325° F	165° C
350° F	180° C
375° F	190° C
400° F	200° C
425° F	220° C
450° F	230° C
475° F	240° C

PREVIEW OF OTHER BOOKS IN THIS SERIES

ESSENTIAL SPICES AND HERBS: TURMERIC

Turmeric is truly a wonder spice. It has anti-inflammatory, antioxidant, anti-cancer, and anti-bacterial properties. Find out the amazing benefits of turmeric. Includes many recipes for incorporating turmeric in your daily life.

Turmeric is a spice known to man for thousands of years and has been used for cooking, food preservation, and as a natural remedy for common ailments. This book explains:

- Many health benefits of turmeric including fighting cancer, inflammation, and pain.
- Turmeric as beauty treatments - turmeric masks
- Recipes for teas, smoothies and dishes
- References and links to a number of research studies on the effectiveness of turmeric

Essential Spices and Herbs: Turmeric is a quick read and offers a lot of concise information. A great tool to have in your alternative therapies and healthy lifestyle toolbox!

PREVENTING CANCER

 World Health Organization (WHO) estimates more than half of all cancer incidents are preventable.

Cancer is one of the most fearsome diseases to strike mankind. There has been much research into both conventional and alternative therapies for different kinds of cancers. Different cancers require different treatment options and offer a different prognosis. While there has been significant progress in recent times in cancer research towards a cure, there are none available currently. However, more than half of all cancers are likely preventable through modifications in lifestyle and diet.

Preventing Cancer offers a quick insight into cancer-causing factors, foods that fight cancer, and how the three spices, turmeric, ginger and garlic, can not only spice up your food but potentially make all your food into cancer fighting meals. While there are many other herbs and spices that help fight cancer, these three spices work together and complementarily. In addition, the medicinal value of these spices has been proven over thousands of years of use. The book includes:

- Cancer-causing factors and how to avoid them.
- Top 12 cancer-fighting foods, the cancers they fight and how to incorporate them into your diet.

- Cancer-fighting properties of turmeric, ginger and garlic
- Over 30 recipes including teas, smoothies and other dishes that incorporate these spices.
- References and links to many research studies on the effectiveness of these spices.

PREVENTING ALZHEIMER'S

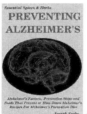
Approximately 50 million people suffer from Alzheimer's worldwide. In the U.S. alone, 5.5 million people have Alzheimer's – about 10 percent of the worldwide Alzheimer's population.

Alzheimer's disease is a progressive brain disorder that damages and eventually destroys brain cells, leading to memory loss, changes in thinking, and other brain functions. While the rate of progressive decline in brain function is slow at the onset, it gets worse with time and age. Brain function decline accelerates, and brain cells eventually die over time. While there has been significant research done to find a cure, currently there is no cure available.

Alzheimer's incidence rate in the U.S. and other western countries is significantly higher than that of the countries in the developing world. Factors such as lifestyle, diet, physical and mental activity, and social engagement play a part in the development and progression of Alzheimer's.

In most cases, if you are above the age of 50, plaques and tangles associated with Alzheimer's may have already started forming in your brain. At the age of 65, you have a 10% chance of Alzheimer's and at age 80, the chances are about 50%.

With lifestyle changes, proper diet and exercise (of the mind and body), Alzheimer's is preventable.

In recent times, Alzheimer's is beginning to reach epidemic proportions. The cost of Alzheimer's to the US economy is expected to cross a trillion dollars in 10 years. It is a serious health care issue in many of the western countries as the population age and the life expectancy increase.

At this time, our understanding of what causes Alzheimer's and the ways to treat it is at its infancy. However, we know the factors that affect Alzheimer's, and we can use that knowledge to prevent, delay the onset or at least slow down the rate of progression of the disease.

While this book does not present all the answers, it is an attempt to examines the factors affecting Alzheimer's and how to reduce the risk of developing Alzheimer's. A combination of diet and both mental and physical exercise is believed to help in prevention or reducing risk. The book includes:

Discussion on factors in Alzheimer's development

The list of foods that help protect the brain and boost brain health is included in the book:

Over 30 recipes including teas, smoothies, broths, and other dishes that incorporate brain-boosting foods:

References and links to several research studies on Alzheimer's and brain foods.

ALL NATURAL WELLNESS DRINKS

 It contains 35 recipes for wellness drinks that include teas, smoothies, soups, and vegan & bone broths. The recipes in this book are unique and combine superfoods, medicinal spices, and herbs. These drinks are anti-cancer, anti-diabetic, ant-aging, heart healthy, anti-inflammatory, and antioxidant as well as promote weight loss.

By infusing nature-based nutrients (super fruits and vegetables, spices, and herbs) into drink recipes, we get some amazing wellness drinks that not only replace water loss but nourish the body with vitamins, essential metals, antioxidants, and many other nutrients. These drinks may be further enhanced by incorporating spices and herbs along with other superfoods. These drinks not only help heal the body but also enhance the immune system to help prevent many forms of diseases. These drinks may also help rejuvenate the body and delay the aging process. The book also includes suggested wellness drinks for common ailments.

ESSENTIAL SPICES AND HERBS: GINGER

Ginger is a spice known to man for thousands of years and has been used for cooking and as a natural remedy for common ailments. Recent studies have shown that ginger has anti-cancer, anti-inflammatory, and antioxidant properties. Ginger helps in reducing muscle pain and is an excellent remedy for nausea. Ginger promotes a healthy digestive system. The book details:

- Many health benefits of ginger including fighting cancer, inflammation, pain and nausea.
- Remedies using ginger.
- Recipes for teas, smoothies, and other dishes
- References and links to a number of research studies on the effectiveness of ginger

ESSENTIAL SPICES AND HERBS: GARLIC

Garlic is one of the worlds healthiest foods. It helps in maintaining a healthy heart, an excellent remedy for common inflections and has both antioxidant and anti-inflammatory properties. It is an excellent food supplement that provides some key vitamins and minerals. This book details the benefits of garlic and describes many easy recipes for incorporating garlic into the diet:

- Many health benefits of garlic including fighting cancer, inflammation, heart health and more.
- Remedies using garlic.
- Recipes for teas, smoothies, and other dishes
- References and links to a number of research studies on the effectiveness of garlic

ESSENTIAL SPICES AND HERBS: CINNAMON

Cinnamon is an essential spice. It has Anti-diabetic, anti-inflammatory, antioxidant, anti-cancer and anti-infections and neuroprotective properties. Cinnamon is a spice known to man for thousands of years and has been used for food preservation, baking, cooking, and as a natural remedy for common ailments. Recent studies have shown that cinnamon has important medicinal properties. This book explains:

- Many health benefits of cinnamon including anti-diabetic, neuroprotective and others.
- Recipes for teas, smoothies, and other dishes
- References and links to a number of research studies on the effectiveness of cinnamon

ANTI-CANCER CURRIES

It is estimated that more than 50% of the cancer incidents are preventable by changing lifestyles, controlling or avoiding cancer-causing factors, or simply eating healthy. There are several foods that are known to have anti-cancer properties either directly or indirectly. Some of these have properties that inhibit cancer cell growth while others have antioxidant and anti-inflammatory properties that contribute to overall health. However, many spices and herbs have direct anti-cancer properties and when one uses anti-cancer spices and herbs in cooking fresh food, there is an immense benefit to be gained. Curry dishes are cooked using many spices that have antioxidant, anti-inflammatory, and anti-cancer properties.

This book contains 30 curry recipes that use healthy and anti-cancer ingredients. These recipes are simple and take an average of 20-30 minutes to prepare.

BEGINNERS GUIDE TO COOKING WITH SPICES

Have you ever wondered how to cook with spices? Learn about the many benefits of spices and how to cook with them!

Find out how to start using spices as seasoning and healthy foods. Includes sample recipes,

Beginner's guide to cooking with spices is an introductory book that explains the history, various uses, and their medicinal properties and health benefits. The book details how they may be easily incorporated in everyday cooking. The book will cover the following:

- Health benefits of spices and herbs
- Spice mixes from around the world and their uses
- Tips for cooking with Spices
- Cooking Vegan with Spices
- Cooking Meat and Fish with spices

- Spiced Rice Dishes
- Spicy Soups and Broths

EASY INDIAN INSTANT POT COOKBOOK

Instant Pot or Electric Pressure Cooker is the most important cooking device in my kitchen. It saves me time, energy, and helps me prepare hassle-free Indian meals all the time.

The Easy Indian Instant Pot Meals contains includes:
- Recipes for 50 Indian dishes
- Tips for cooking with Instant Pot or any electric pressure cooker
- General tips for cooking with spices

FIGHTING THE VIRUS: HOW TO BOOST YOUR BODY'S IMMUNE RESPONSE AND FIGHT VIRUS NATURALLY

What can we do to improve our health and immune response so that our bodies are less prone to viral or bacterial infections? How can we enable our body for a speedy recovery in case of getting such infections?

The answer lies in lifestyle changes that include better hygiene

practices, exercise, sleep, and a better diet to keep our body in optimum health. This book is focused on understanding the body's immune system, factors that improve the body's immune response and some natural remedies and recipes. The book contains:
•Overview of the human immune system
•Factors affecting immune response
•Natural substances that fight viral, fungal and bacterial infections
•Recipes that may improve immunity and help speedy recovery
•Supplements that may help improve the immune system
•Scientific studies and references.

EASY SPICY EGGS: ALL NATURAL EASY AND SPICY EGG RECIPES

 Recipes in this book are not a collection of authentic dishes, but a spicy version of chicken recipes that are easy to make and 100% healthy and flavorful. Ingredients used are mostly natural without any preserved or processed foods.

Most of these recipes include tips and tricks to vary and adapt to your taste of spice level or make with some of the ingredients you like other than the prescribed ingredients in the recipes.

There are about 30 recipes in the book with ideas to make another 30 or even more with the suggestions and notes included with many of the recipes. Cooking does not have to be prescriptive but can be creative. I invite you to try your own variations and apply your creativity to cook dishes that are truly your own.

FOOD FOR THE BRAIN

Nature provides for foods that nourish both the body and the brain. Most often the focus of the diet is physical nourishment, - muscle building, weight loss, energy, athletic performance, and many others. Similar to foods that help the body, there are many foods that help the brain, improve memory and help slow down the aging process. While it is normal to have your physical and mental abilities somewhat slow down with age, diseases such as Alzheimer's, and Parkinson's impact these declines even more. Brain function decline accelerates, and more and more brain cells eventually die over time.

With regular exercises, strength training, practicing martial arts and other physical activities can arrest the physical decline. This book's primary focus is on managing decline in mental and brain function through diet and contains the following:
Characteristics of foods that helps in keeping your brain healthy and young. Brain healthy foods including meats, fruits, vegetables, spices, herbs, and seafood. Supplements to improve memory, cognition and support brain health
Mediterranean diet recipe ideas
DASH diet recipe ideas
Asian diet recipe ideas
Brain boosting supplements and recommendations products and dosage
References.